tourmaline

tourmaline

ginger tran

*to the past,
present,
and future*

contents .

***

*

natural progression

there is always the nothingness

that first comes, first serves.

then the everythingness that blossoms

like microscopic fireworks

if you lean in real closely

to the very tips of things –

like bushes and trees, and the entire

tunneling out of known space and time.

when it's still dark out

you just have to stick with it
to see the scale tip to the other side.

it's too early in the show right now
to think you know the final scene.

everything is stretched out in time
too vast for us to really see.

but if you sink below it, if you are still
within the boundlessness of it,

you can feel it.

you can feel the gradient of your life
being sprinkled with bits of white.

you can sense the immensity of what
you still have yet to comprehend.

that it is left unfurled for you already;
you just have to decide

to keep choosing what can only
be paced, what will only seem

arduous at first, but what will
ultimately push you to the verge

of where the sun will rise.

over and over again, you must choose
not to hide.

oxidation

art and expression
is the immediate
mending up of
what you allow
to spill out –
to split yourself apart
and have the rawness
of it all touch air.
because the oxidation
of all wounds
is all that is needed
to allow the healing
of oneself to start
the healing process
on its own.
and that is where
beauty merges with
and is emerged from.

self-psychology

keep reminding yourself
that it is the unburdening
of your damaged psyche

that now needs to find
it's own way
of perceiving reality

through many re-visitations
and uncomfortable letting gos;

it's what you must know
when this journey
starts to take its toll.

*

opening

depression happens when
there is an over-connectivity
in our brains;
it is not the lack of feelings.
but rather, feeling so much
that the mind mistakes it
for an intruder.
in which it has to protect itself
against. to be immune
to such heaviness. from carrying
the weight of all the states
of yous that you experience.
the pounds of all the lives
you unknowingly soak up
from others. the millions
of neuronal streamlines
flooding the doorway
that directs a river out
into the open sea.
it is there
for us to see
what and how much we really need.
to exhale longer
than that which we take in.
to expand the infrastructure
of our experience
by relocating blockades.
to not perpetuate this gouging
out of ourselves from what we
are frightened will be too much
for us to handle.
stay with it. it gets better.

ethereal / germinating

just because it is invisible
does not mean that it is not real.

it sometimes fades
out of sight but that doesn't mean
you shouldn't hold space for it
to come back, manifold.

it hides but that doesn't mean
it's still not there
waiting to show up.

it can't be adequately articulated,
but it doesn't mean it can't be spoken to;

doesn't mean it doesn't secretly
speak to you
in languages your verbal mind
can't comprehend.

you are keeping it
to yourself right now,
and that's alright.

because you are understanding
how it feels
for invisibility
to navigate old lurid worlds.

you are significantly listening
for when crown kisses air
and sunlight,

*

and for how and when
you can start
living in the spaces
between it all.

absolute freedom

as if to blend in with your surroundings

makes it so that you could more easily live.

as if making gentle creaks on wooden floors

threatens the exposure of your neediness.

needs to be heard and to be present and to be held

up by something like the ground and the earth.

as if that is just too much to ask: to just be alive.

you need more than believing your un-weight

will naturally bring more rightness than wrong.

you deserve more than tiptoeing the lines

between self-starvation and absolute freedom.

*

anti-dispersion / anti-ptsd

the blood and the nerves
all rushing away from your limbs
are backing down
from an invisible fight.

to find peace again
in your organs and inner system;
it will take some getting use to.

this tingling of stillness.
this fullness of being.
this literal feel-ing of your insides
has never been more unnerving,
yet so necessary
to know such deep rest again.

iceberg

when you are used to
diving into depths this deep,
holding your breath to
sink down further to
sink in faster,
it gets easier
and easier
to know how to plummet,
to taste the salt
and to nestle yourself
on the ocean floor.
you forget all about the pressure
that is water above you,
surrounding you
and crushing you
because
the depression of your lungs
and the melancholic high
enables you to feel closer
to the backbone you wish you had
to lean on
in someone or something else.

*

nausea

it is not the lack of contents
in your stomach that is making
this dry heave impossible
to throw anything up.
but the emptiness in the pit of you,
the scar tissue of where your roots
were marred. it is the center
of yourself that was not allowed
any warmth or bit of recognition,
and the cold air of its absence
is making its way through you,
like wind through hollow chimes.
signaling to you, you've been made
to be unreal for all this time.

t h r o w i t
a l l u p.

sobriety

for now, dreams can be perfectly ok.
you can snuggle up to them like a blanket.
but you must learn to distinguish
eventually
those dreams you know will never be,
from the dreams that might just could be,
then from the dreams that will inevitably be.

no matter which though, they will never
turn out the same in reality.
the point of dreams is to capture
and make more sober
the feelings you are after
rather than what you see.

they serve as fleeting signposts,
leaving behind the ghosts
of their emotional shapes –

the trick comes down to learning
how to not be swayed by images,
but to discern its common residual flavors.
so for now, dreams can be perfect
and they are ok when
you don't let them lead you
entirely astray.

vortex

the universe is taking you with it,
back into the place it came from.
expand and contract and contract
and expand until you are but
a seedling again, enough to grow
roots that communicates with
the whole. underground network.
you are aiding in the death
and rebirth of something far grander
than you, but also solely just for you.
something magnificent, to stand
in place of that which does not belong
anymore. that which is only trying to
circumnavigate its many jeweled facets.
to grasp more of what it really is
before taking the plunge again
into complete unknown reinvention.
the universe is taking you with it,
and you need to make the decision
to be swept up and swept down into,
to help the both of you.

wavelengths

what we see in our minds' eye
never quite aligns with where
our hearts stand in real time.

the conscious and the unconscious always
needs time to be aware of the other,
and for those rare moments of clarity,
embraces the dollops of each other entirely.

what you can rationalize to yourself
does not mean your lesson is learned.
it only beckons you to keep putting in the work
you need to do to shorten the shadow
between you and the much realer you.

it takes patience and consistency.
it means for you to quietly plant seeds
in the parts of your yet to be healed
psyche, where your soul is dying
to ignite and flourish out from.

it means for you to learn what color
you are sowing and what colors you need
to really weave together the wavelength
of light that shines through little by little.

guan yin

something of a protection
as she swept down from space,
illuminating like the moon
on a black night.

she sat cross-legged on thin air
outside your window frame.

a silent smile she graced.
warm. handed you a lotus.
pink. and a calendar you hung
on your wall.

the volatile numbness you would feel
in the upcoming years would be born
out of your sole need to survive.

seeded in this was
the echo of that dream
you now know
could've only been a sign:

the objects given to you
telling you to be patient,
that everything that thrives
out of the impossible
always just needs its time.

fervor, not fever

born with a dancer's delicateness –
your thin ankles and birdlike feet
were always too ready
to just fly away.

as if you could not let your divinity
permeate your whole body,
to reach down to the soles
of your feet, to be stood in.

there will always be those who
are too afraid of the ones who
generate too much electricity.

but this is not something to keep
to yourself, and it is not something
that can be easily stolen out
from underneath you.

the safe haven you preciously maintain
to travel back and forth to and from
needs to be the wings, excavated,
that flees you, not from yourself
or your experience,
but from this nest you've found yourself in.

after all, your true fear
is that you really just might be able
to make that happen.

*

gasp of air

these are only shock waves
jolting you alive.
you are being resuscitated.
you are doing the resuscitating.

these are only shock waves
jolting you alive.
you are being resuscitated.
you are doing the resuscitating.

these are only shock waves
jolting you alive.
you are being resuscitated.
you are doing the resuscitating.

these are only shock waves.
these are only shock waves.
these are only shock waves.
these are only shock waves.

cellular memory

get in touch with your muscles
and get in touch with your joy.
one day the two will meet
and remember each other.

symbiosis celebrated.

ribcage

your ribcage
already protects
your heart.

don't feel like you need
to rampage
and build a castle around
what is already a home for you.

that would just mean
you are constantly having to live
on the outskirts of your self
to do so.

nights spent in confusion

when you find yourself
in bed
saying, whimpering, crying
i don't know
what is happening to me…
know that it is love
breaking you open, darling.
because love is seeping through.
using the forces you've
mentally kept at bay
to sew you up
into that long,
hidden, awaiting core.

lightness

you felt bad for the things
that were meant to feel good
about.

as if you didn't deserve
such lightness.

you decided it was much
better to say
you didn't deserve the good
than it was to realize
maybe you just didn't know
how to let those things in
just yet.

to punish yourself for
something that was never
your fault.
when you were simply taught
to not trust
in the bigger scope of you.

you were on high alert for
what was scattered
sporadically for you –
tiny morsels of the only love
you knew.

from shaky hands you had
to hold
but was made to feel
that it was not.

to have the kind of love
you then wanted for yourself
felt crippling
and threatening,
because it would expose so much
of who you have yet to become,
or more so, who
you have to leave behind.

don't feel bad
for the masks you wore
and the masks that worked.

the glow of such lightness
will always be able to breathe through.
like strong green vines
that grow and thicken
to their densest
when you begin to let
vacant sites
rust in delight over time.

*

the line between thinking and knowing

the line between delusion and clarity can be so faint.
because we are able to see both so vividly in some way.
so maybe to push forward, all we need is the audacity
to be a tad bit insane either way.

crazy enough to try to bring change into fruition.
by learning to discern whether you are crazily spiraling
into the vacuum of your mind, or crazily spiraling out
from the love uncovered within your heart.
that fine distinguishing, i guess, is all you really need.

the worry over being delusional no longer matters when
the instinct behind it is to courageously expand from rather
than the mere excuses to accumulate to stay stagnant in.

beyond what pain can ever deceive

at one point, the pain you feel
will cease to feel like suffering.

like a burden that is always
tormenting you. plunging you towards
your most fought against nightmares.

in the near future, the crying will begin
to feel more like propulsion
for your courageous tunnel trekking.

seated fetal shell, pulsating seed
needed to receive
self-implanting answers.
your prayers gently accelerating
the overcoming and transformation
of all these obstacles.

at one point the loneliness will cease
to look like evidence of you being
a fragile broken piece,

and will start to feel like a no longer
kept resistance to deep necessary
solitude – the only soft ignition
that can heal and guide you back
to wholeness.

inter and intra connectedness.
beyond what pain can ever deceive.

*

crime it did not commit

don't hold it against your body
for what it had to come into contact with.

you cannot continue to compensate
for not having had the ability
to control what happened in the past
by now having restrictive control
of your ever-present –

ever-streaming
every second of every day.

you think by punishing and beating out
the toxicity from inside you,
that it will bring you relief, or a sense
of correcting rights from wrongs,
but you have to know
there was nothing toxic inside of you
to begin with.

your body only wants
to regain the emotional freedom
from the crime it did not commit.

slopping heart

as you lay upon your side,
your slopping heart
unwound,

a spiral of escape
for one minute
becomes unbound.

immersive and immense.
let the sloshing begin.
let the breaths breathe their own.
let the knees curl in.

so that for a minute,
the eyes can
perceive home.

this indentation
on your side will not be
for very long;

lean into it.

astral projective fear

it is only when you are resistant
to something that you are susceptible
to its overwhelming influence.

the being that once kept you alive
is still in some ways alive, and if you treat it
as if it has died, it will cling onto its life.

emerging activities from unwanted ghosts.

quiet

quiet feelings obscured
by the need to be
emotionally conveying,
and truthfully ingraining.

you haven't yet learned
how to not take offense
at irreparable
blind-and-deafness.

nothing
needs to be carved
into a mountain
to be truly witnessed;

this bleeding
over yourself
only compromises
your own sanity.

*

erasing the chalk

i know your habit
of freezing moments because
the world had made
its own habit
of pronouncing them dead.

so you've been trying to encase
in chalk
what you were adamant
were all its forms.

i know they are only attempts
to preserve and
even stubbornly keep alive
these fragments of your truths.

though i want you now to feel
the need not to defend
your every ounce of life anymore.
to live it
instead of gathering evidence
that it is there. (it. is. there.)

because to submerge yourself
in detail and having a mile long
explanation for an inch
keeps you from mending
the split up-ness that was torn.

because to fragment
the fragmented
out of sticking to a conviction
keeps you from truly
moving forward.

sifting

it is not enough
to merely call it
soul searching anymore.

it is soul revelation.
individual revolution.
molecular awakening.

like all that is not needed
being moved around
for the site of gold.

the witnessing of your body
being, looking up at your skin
breathing, moves you.
and is how you can hear
the multi-layers
of your clandestine heart –

with its years of yearning,
stretching, and brimming
with the need to be trusted in.

the glistening thing to be caught
and discovered this time
because you were sifting for it
to come through.

it is what has always been there.
waiting in disguise.
until your softening allows it
to take hold of you
like it once had before.

*

so it is not enough
to merely see it
as soul searching anymore…

because you do not go looking for it
as if it were lost.
you start allowing it
to reveal
its many faces.

force of will

i can feel you secretly
wanting to close off this opening
happening within you.

i can sense you battling
with whether this expanse is false or not.
whether this shift towards hope
is a delusion or not.

you sometimes think
all this inward seeking and higher
knowing is just sprouted
from your rapid imagination.

but let me tell you,
what imagination is,
is the ground that makes fertile
your dreams, desires, and needs.

your playground to paint brushstrokes on
before the final piece.
childlike but not child's play.

imagination makes what creation
is privileged with,
and you have been wanting
more than anything,
to create the life you were not given,
but still the life that you
have always been meant for.

i know everyone says
you should be afraid of heights.
but the ideal of what is comfortable
and ignorant will not stop
what has started, even if you try.

*

and let's be honest,
you have never felt safe anywhere anyway –
yet you've survived.
so let's not pretend
that safety is what you are really after.

rainforest magic

what you want
is building up for you
on the other side.

waiting for this path
to be taken.
waiting for vegetation
to be cut through.
for opaque waters
to be made into ripples.

the dark night
will only grow darker,
until you can see
that acclimating
is the only way
to feel your way
through it all.

until what bursts into sight
is better than sureness,
better than what comes easily,
better than staying in one place.

what you want
knows your heart
needs to beat
to different sounds
to keep alive.

spiral

sometimes to be more open
is to know when to close yourself off.
to be open to the integration
of needing little, so that the little
that is needed can regain
composure and gently sprout.

to know that the former opening
you thought was your savior,
now is just the freedom
that was feigned in favor
of your escapist flavor.

because to spin a web from a designated
point is always the hardest to choose.
but it must be chosen, and you must
narrow in on it. because perhaps
you knew where it was and where
it had to come from all along,
but the circles you ran around it
seemed all you could do at the time.

now you know those kinds of circles
vanish quickly after the dust settles,
and the one that is worth anything
is the one you forge only from within
your center. that is how all flowers,
seashells, and galaxies form anyway.

fruit

underneath the urge to destroy
is the very real sense of searching
for something new.

we make the mistake of thinking
that to destroy means we want nothing
left in our wake. that it signifies
a kind of malady or evil in us.

but that only comes from people
who don't understand
the need for immense change.

we don't want nothing,
no.
we want beyond the confines
of something
that no longer bears fruit.

**

throb

that throbbing in your heart?

let it
reverberate into
all your bloodstreams
and channels.
until all your fingers
and toes
feel recirculated.
until all the tears
in your eyes
are unloaded.
and until you can sink
into your throned seat
at the center of your core.

that throbbing… is nothing
but vibration
aiming to reorganize
all the cells in your body,
to transmute them
into a higher and freer,
more wondrous
state of being.

spine

sometimes i remember me facing upward –
resigned –
engrossed in white walls –
frozen –
as if i could just melt into the white oblivion.

but then i remember quite concretely
you pushing me onto my stomach,
pulling down my garments, revealing me,
climbing on top of me.

and i realize now the real possibility
of me fully rearranging my insides
to zone in on just what was happening;
aware but detached,
some form of control but controlled,

as if i could protect a part of myself
by literally watching my own back –

twisted mind
for lack of a twisted spine;

the glaciers are cracking now
and i feel every creak, trying to
twist back around –

**

collapse

disappearance:
a silent explosion,
catastrophic
in the night sky.
death of a star.
the exponential pink and blue
and green emersion
tightening your own existence,
or shining from
the evaporation of it.
you fall into yourself.
out of view –
a rabbit hole. a wormhole.
a whole eternity,
triggered in
a millisecond.

rest in peace

your pain keeps bringing you back
because you are unfinished with it.

there is still more to understand,
still more to pay respect to;

the dead isn't dead until you know
why it is you have to say goodbye.

why it is not for you to carry anymore
as if it were still alive.

make peace with it and cry…
however much you need to.

but know, you both deserve to rest now.
in your respective spots. please, lie gently.

**

magma

breathe
into
your open
wounds.
you are more
than
you'll ever
know.
let the hurt
erupt
over
your barren
land
and the cooled
lava
will be
marvelous –
your thickened
scar tissues
will form
mountains
only you
can climb
over.
crystallizing
what
only you
can see.
minerals for
the most
enriching
soil:
fertile ground

you will
persist on.

the eye of it

who told you that hurricanes
look the same on the inside
as it does from the out.

who brainwashed you into thinking
you would lose all control
if you gave in, even just a little.

who confiscated your will to take
the first step into the whirling
masses that are calling out for you.

sprinkling holy showers of love
your way.
melting the armor in your dreams
as you keep resisting.

who told you time would not stand still
or work in your favor
once you relinquish yourself to it.

to be in the midst of all
that is uprooting
for your smooth renewal.

you will see in the eye of it
that everything moves in slow motion,
becomes atoms you could touch
and rearrange.

and when you are no longer
sidetracked by the places
you need to be, it will place you
safely right down
where you belong.

**

existential loneliness

i've lit myself on fire
every day for years
to keep from feeling
the loneliness
of my own
existential core.

to not know why
anything at all mattered,
because i didn't know how
i, myself,
could possibly matter
was confusion
my little self couldn't take.
so to escape,

i laughed the loudest,
cried the hardest,
slept the deepest,
to keep from feeling
the trauma of my bare skin
keeping me on my own,
the sound of my heart exposed
and echoing into distances,
the movement of all
that was inside me,
working, and reminding me
i still had me
to deal with.

i didn't know
that potent emptiness
enabled the location
of vibrations
for new things
to arise.

so little by little,
i stopped trying to escape,
stopped trying to ignore
that deep unrest in me;
the expanse i felt
my soul inhabit
when i was (painfully) still,
when i experienced
the tears down my face
and the blood in my veins
as unrelenting rivers
forging way.

**

ghosts

a tantrum cloaked in love.
the solace of two flames
licking each other's wounds;
it fit as an escape.

7 months and my ghost
was showing – my form:
only a reflection of you.
my kisses: a deflection

of my incapacity to be seen.
planting visions on your face
with my lips – sweet seeming
promises watered from

our longing
to make it real.

root energy

maybe you haven't been connecting
to people from your rootedness at all,
because you haven't yet known
what real rootedness feels like.

maybe you've been only connecting
to the idea of people, manipulating
your energies and theirs to create
the right kind of scenario from your mind.

maybe experiencing them as human was hard
because to be reminded you were one also
could place you in danger of hurting like one,
and being betrayed by any one of them.

but we have all been there before. we've all
been so afraid of being fully within ourselves
that we either hover just above our bodies
or pulverize the cement with our bare feet.

because we've all known the fragility
of earthly life – the unexpected uprootedness.
impermanence that shocks. we've let
others bury in us, and us in them, pulling at

each other's strings to weave safety blankets
for ourselves. not wanting to lose nor shed.
though one needs to go underground in order
to really connect. and connecting isn't

constant hoarding. of saving people
and things before they can even be lost.
no one really disappears if you are rooted.
to root is to be with all and to be with all

**

doesn't necessarily yield obvious closeness,
or being attached at the site of germination.
you no longer have to compromise love
with invaded space. or truth with isolation.

because of reveries

she understood me.
yes, she understood
all the things that i showed.
but what i didn't
understand was
the open cave below,
in which so much more
had been neglected
to be explored.
so yes, she and i believed
in the me i wanted to be,
instead of the actual churning
of the rawer world aching
underneath –
slimy lack of premeditation,
underestimated since
that is where real abilities lie.
only through pain and drudgery.
these aren't given chances
to be seen
if you are constantly bound
by overwhelming reveries.

**

it's a pixel

to let go
without abandoning.

because to abandon
is to make a gap,

and there needn't be
more gaps created

when you are trying
to make yourself

whole.

skin of others

i can feel myself sometimes
pouring into people
all because deep down i need
to be filled.

and by knowing how to project
and amplifying absorption,
i can feel
their filled in-ness.

i can feel some presence
wanting to give to them
the way i want to be
given to.

their memories glow
under my skin.
i've lived
in the information of others.

**

scavenger

sometimes i eat my dinner
with the intent of gorging
on something i am eager
to swallow.

i find myself searching
instantaneously for all the avenues
of satiation i can attain
in this piece of chocolate cake.

i find myself bent and draped
over this strip of chicken,
hungrily in the space of desiring
to be the one consumed –

to be overwhelmed,
to reach a state i had in mind.
to feel relief, to feel the warmth,
to feel what i don't want to feel inside.

instead of letting the taste fall
delicately on my tongue,
i race to catch it in its tracks,
before it can really make an impact.

the moment is gone within seconds,
yet my head still spins and is alert
for what it failed to find
in the center of my plate.

edge of the horizon

a ring around my head
was swelling with things
i couldn't yet grasp,
like the edge of the horizon
when the sun is quivering
before undoubtedly descending
into a place we don't know.
your absence makes me
want to disappear
into a place
i do know,
and don't want ever again
to go –
i'm begging the abrupt
darkness
to just let go.
please,
go.

**

regressive

what you fear most is fear itself.
not the object
of what is causing you fear.

but the fear that you will collapse
into yourself.

the fear that you have no barriers
strong enough to hold you
all together.

no grand deity possibly invested
in keeping you alive.

you fear you will become
the child
that was abandoned again.

it is the fear of being vulnerable
that causes your outrage.
it is the reaction to fear
that causes this turmoil.

not fear itself.

embrace
fear.

give it the soothing
it needs. then slowly
help it back
onto its feet.

birthday

cake is smeared on her lips,
or at least,
the regurgitation of it.

she dances inside her head,
frothed in white,
like the cream on top.

she sings a song,
but her throat is too raw
and tongue too stuck

from keeping in
what she should let out,
from keeping down

to keep from showing up.
i handle her gently,
and lead her to bed.

she is sweet, but barely there,
she is love, but cannot bare.
i wait for her to wake up.

**

hymnal

you, the black torso
of a butterfly,

head lowered modestly –
you, you sing to yourself.

is it the myth, that
pigs can't look up at the sky?

can butterflies not see their own
majestic wings, sprawled

and equivalent to the reign
of a brown eagle?

one flap, one blow,
can cause a whole tornado.

you are red, you are blue,
you are pink and yellow,

and dotted, with veins
like a stained glass

green tara, vibrating loudly
in a quiet monastery.

antithesis of a supernova

i wanted to swallow your abyss;

i quietly tipped
and toed my way around,
pressed myself up
against you in our slumber

and in my daze –
i wanted to be that pebble
in your crack, preventing
the whole of you to collapse.

but was it me who was caving in?
black holes that know nothing but consume.
when i let you

across my horizon, event,
festive,
i instilled in you
the thing i wanted to be shown in me.

because how we learned to love
was to create an image of it,
to be safely protected from within.

but we know a gravity
with too much mass and too much longing
only elicits you
to keep falling, and falling

into that disappearing diamond in the sky.

i wanted to taste your lips
i wanted to(o)
much.

**

boundaries

ask yourself:

how can i be my own person
within the realms
of my own bounds.

and not lose myself in others
as a way to connect
or to keep them around.

etheric disconnection

it was impossible for her
not to live in her mind.
with her eyes scrunched up
so tight. in dreams
where she could play
out all the feelings
she wished she could feel
during the day.

not because she wanted
to keep out the light.
but because she needed
to hold on to any bit of it.
because even though
the moments and the routines
are not filled with danger now,
they are still
too heavy to process, still
too amped up in the adrenaline
that was carried over.

and even though the beds,
and the floors,
and all the walls
have been swept up in change,
she still touched everything
with the same body
that remembered for her.
because all darkness
had been found to feel the same –
reminders of something
she once,
twice,
several times
couldn't have any control over.

**

(disconnected bodies tend to feel like
electronic devices you have no knowledge
of fixing. one you can't easily reboot
to not glitch again. and to not make
erratic noises anymore. signaling impulses
to you you'd rather not have to receive.)

with her mind up so high
and the rest of her body
pushed out of sight,
she left her heart
in a state of confusion.
incessantly reaching out to
any and all counterparts,
not excluding what wasn't hers.

this state of limbo felt good
at the time. she was not asleep.
and neither yet dead.
just an open gash she
could cover up with a blanket.
her etheric body buried
in different worlds
to numb out the pain.

stuck in the bounds, she was,
of something her childhood
self could not believe
and did not understand.

hypervigilance

you can, for this moment,
let yourself know
that you can rest
from what your mind
involuntarily does best.

**

facets

the eons that have passed that have made
this journey so familiar. the lives lived
amongst stars and watery rocks provide
all the dualities you have to mend now.
asteroids that you had to collide with
on your way across the galaxy. those dents
on your surfaces may as well be called
the shimmering facets of the diamond
that came from all those dense moments.
to have landed where you are now. you
have been here before but in another era.
this is not something you have to struggle
and fight against, but something to recall
and unfold again with more vigor this time.
you have been here before but the universe
keeps on turning its axis for you. to gain
more footing. moons to illuminate your orbit.

voices beneath water

it's not about knowing
how to hear
super crisply and clearly.
it's about learning
how to drown
out all the noise.
and let
what was always there
speaking to you
rise to conscious surface
to finally
be acknowledged.

**

what arises is now safe to arise

don't be afraid of the manic
voices telling you what you
ought to do. they are not
like before: reducing space
instead of finding and pushing
limits for it.

these are the ones in you
who compiles clouds, and arranges
webs of stars for you to fall
toward something and be caught
this time.

because they know
that you have known
that free floating scare
of being deep in outer space before.
without a harness, and without
a voice telling you, you're doing alright.

and so it's okay that you've sought
all angles, and know what tables
to not bump into.
it's okay that you are looking
over your shoulders one too many times.
it's okay that you are hammering
in lessons that you have yet
to come across right now.

we know that figuring out the basics
is the first step we need in order
to let ourselves free fall
into this wonderful contraption of ours,
able to return always
to center and center and center again.

and what arises will be safe to arise.

**

night owl logic

we only come out in the night
when we are not fully comfortable
with being seen in the light.

our spirits congested –
only waiting for when it is quiet

to bring out of us the world,
for which we were told
there was no room.

to forgive

the goodness that you thought
you had screwed up
and lived to be without
is naturally always going
to be there, ready
and willing.

it is just as resilient
as your ability to forgive
yourself for believing
you were wrong.
for giving into all
the outside voices
telling you, you were off track.

lost faith and abandoned
compassion and absent hope
always finds some opening
in grounds where everything
seems to be buried;

it is that stubborn.
and it will never be
in the places you think it is.
because the search for it
cultivates the greatest find
of them all:
that patience
is your most
fundamental
searchlight.

natural medicine

you are never doing
too little. this is
open heart surgery.

this is gentle energy
swooning in this time
to cradle you.

you have an idea.
you have an inkling.
you know
what is happening.

there is no chaos
needing to be slayed
here. you are
potently surrendering.

hibernation

it is a survival mechanism to hide out
for a while. but as the winds calm,
the ultimate survival instinct
always kicks in
to override it somehow.

we are the ones who gently pat
our dreams on the back each night
like babies who need
soft reassurance
on their mothers' chests.

we are the ones who happily drown
in that sea of envisioned liberation,
so that when the time comes,
we will know
how to not panic under it.

there is a biological drive
in those of us who can remember
that this waking life is not
the most potent one.

if we can surrender
to the small in us, who is actually
the bigger in us,
the thing we've stowed away
for safekeeping all this time,
we can begin to reestablish
the connection
and to re-braid

our minds.
bodies.
and souls.

**

tomorrow is here

that is the myth:
if there isn't much external
recognition, then there is
nothing more to it.

the outside noise is the thing
that beckons you to want
this over and done with.
to prematurely harvest
when the season isn't over yet.

but the inside voice knows
this is something to be
reveled in. something so
delicious in its serene
unknowingness.

you will know that this is
not being done to you –
this silencing that can feel
at first like pointless
torture –
but that this is being done
for you.

the idea of completing
a journey is just in the mind.
we are already complete;
but we've strayed from this fact.
and the journey, in fact,
is to come to reveal it
again.
and again.

because your own sense of worth
becomes a thing of your own
creation. and creating
has secretly been
what you've always done best.

**

parasites

you are the host.

conditions are parasites
you have to learn
to wean away from
without risking all the blood
to pour from you
by just ripping them off.

just as you've been conditioned
to steer away from
all authentic expressions,
you also have to learn again,
through trial and error,
what it means to be real.

how to exist

when you've been taught not to.
when you've gone through years
not in the process
of exposing
your most tender, hidden self.

it takes time, and guts
to stomach the site
of yourself bleeding.
it takes discernment
and some heartache
carefully extracting all the voices
that have unconsciously embedded themselves
in your head.

black out

i was empty
when i stood up.

you caught me mid-black out
in a lie, where then i woke the fuck up.

capsule

droplets of memories:
the miniscule swirls
of the faces and backgrounds
that are liquid
enough to taste
on the tip of your tongue
yet vast enough
to trace
back to the distinct
magnified universe you
cradled inside yourself
at that
strange point in time.

warm, wet, and neon-like.

capsule (ii)

the sweetest high
comes from the sugar
you coat on top of it.
you are tripping
on your mind's
alteration of events.
memories are but
the last flavor
you add into it.

make note of it
    and move on.

**

the virtue of sensitivity

be grateful that the softness
in your belly
can form strands
to be tightly woven
together to filter
what you are growing
to recognize
does not belong in your body
any longer.

musings of the heart

go ahead and try all directions.
and when none of them will give you
what you need, know
that you still have a place
to come home to. we are here
waiting for you.

the foreign language of the heart
is a tongue not firstly
recognized, yet it is the one
that most deliciously slips
off our lips when we try.

and it is something we've muted
for far too long
because the journey to it
seems laden with thorns.
and the mimicry of it
instead is something easier
to cope with.

we've staved off the real muscles
of it because this too obvious,
too out of control, too vulnerable
spotlight stands at the entrance,
searing right into our too real
yet hidden existence before
we are let in.

all this emotional flesh, meat,
and organs of ours seems on display.
susceptible to being prey.
because the headlights we were
once disturbed with
has kept us frozen in place.

**

though the flames we've ignited
to feel
some sort of aliveness
never makes it through the night.
and we know we haven't been able
to stop
oscillating back and forth. back
and forth between
hardening and scattering about.

so go ahead and try all directions.
and when none of them
will give you peace, know
that the journey home
will be laden with excitement
disguised as apprehension,
and intuition disguised
as insanity.

but there is a place
beyond the misshaped fears,
and we are here
waiting for you.

feel you i

i feel god when i trace
my fingers over the smooth
skin of my belly.

i feel god when i lick my lips
and go
into a trance when dancing.

i feel god when i open my windows
at night and hear
the seductive quietness –
staticky commotion.

i feel god when the sun manages to slip
like silk through the clouds, kissing
the parts of me it can catch.

i feel god when i can show you
me, which isn't as often as i like.

i feel god when i fall deeper
into witnessing my forgotten selves,
which is happening more,
in a way i do like.

i feel god in these cells of mine
that allow me to feel, in that small
window of time where ordinary
and extraordinary intermix.

i feel god in between radiating bodies,
and in the attentive yet empty corners,
peaking their ears out towards us.

**

bridge it

remember that you are
where you are,
and that the high thrill
or fret to get
where you need to be
need not be
so consumed so rapidly,

that there is still
a gap you must
be comfortable with
in order to bridge it,
and to carry the delicate
weight of the unknown,

to arrive a different person
than the one
you thought
was supposed to be.

surprise yourself.

unsticking the masks

it was supposed to be for protection.
and it was. until we meet ourselves
in the dark, and see
too many times that these masks
are doing more harm now
than good.

it was supposed to be experimentation.
temptation to get by unscathed.
it once gave us an image
of a face
we deemed more valuable
than the one we couldn't
stand to get to know.

it was supposed to be for defense.
just for a little while.
until we've come to see that everything
has suddenly become a reason
to be involuntarily
defended against. helpless
to what we've created.

**

what keeps saving me

love…
pure energy and pure enthusiasm.
needing rise, needing friction.
to carve itself out into multilayered
folding outwardly soft petals.

love…
embracer of chaos and encourager
of truth. never able to be caught
though. only gently experienced.
always stepping in when welcomed.

love…
inspiration requiring life. in constant
motion. seeking out who will serve
it best, who can hear it beyond words,
who will find ways to free it at last.

the shape of sound

…and all at once the song changes you.

you give into the onset of no control.
the space beyond the space you are standing in.
where the pitted part inside of you lifts, as if
you are worshipping complete intangible sound.
reminding you of places you've never been,
placing you inside bodies you've never lived.
and you're not sure if all of you is hurting,
or if you're just being flung across the universe,
at the speed of light, where things slow down
and this is where you become unstuck.
pulsating in two places at once. if this is how
the rawness of capitulated movement feels.
exceptionally caught in airy waves that splash
up against your insides, showing you how
your body is shaped, the way bats see
and find their way through black unlit caves.
and you give up the battle between winning
or losing because… none of it matters
when this is all what anyone really wants:

is just to be moved. and to move. and move…

**

eternal recurrence

if everything is a cycle,
if your emptiness is a cycle,
if the darkness is what you
keep returning back to,
then know,
that so is your joy.
so is that love you feel
inside yourself opening up
more and more, little by little.
so is the natural current then
that unceasingly washes you back
to the familiar grounds
of your wildly
unrelenting
beaconed heart.

stark naked

the moment comes
when you're going to have to
let yourself rise

from the ash
instead of just meandering
in the inspection
and dissection of it.

no reward is reaped
in rewinding or editing
yourself down.

(re)birth celebrates
the mess, the nakedness.
all the things nobody
is prepared for,
yet manage anyway.

and perhaps you were not
made to feel you would be
loved
for your messiness.
so this seems hard.

so know that naturally
you are loved. and maybe
this will be easy.

**

the worst of it

the worst of it is over now.

but it still means we have to sit with the havoc that it wreaked. it still means we have to go around picking up the pieces, trying to salvage the salvageable, and seeing what we can mend and what we cannot.

the pertinent points that categorizes such a destruction may no longer be here, but we sit in its wake all the same. we sit here, stupefied for a little bit, disoriented for a little bit, still weighed down by the mess that rearranged our nervous systems a little bit. it takes a while to collect ourselves and most importantly, to start facing the reality that things will never be the same again.

but that in itself doesn't have to be a bad thing. we can't go back to the same life we were leading, because as you can see, the floorboards are already torn up. that phase has passed. it is always going to be the road with all the signs pointing to a second life now. that is your true north now. everything is waiting for your ground to grow with more fertility this time.

there is a heaviness that such chaos brings, yes... but it can be clipped into paper birds and paper airplanes to be flung out, leaving lightness for yourself and breadcrumbs for others. it can be a snowing of what has survived.

the worst of it is over now. but it just means we are only beginning to want more. to carve better for ourselves.

***

moreness

maybe all that you are is more
than all the things you are not.

and maybe you've got to start to trust
the uncertainty of discovering
this moreness rather than obliging to
who you were told you were not
and should act like instead.

the weight of all that you aren't
is easily seeable. but the glorious
abundance of all that you are
can only be felt, and relinquished into.

the unknown

sometimes the most foreign
territory is also the place
you come to feel
is so strangely familiar.

when you let all your senses
and quiet moments of awe
captivate you,

they simultaneously pull you
and instill in you
the wonder of whether

this is merely the path of land
you might have just forgotten
and have now come again to know
so dearly this time around.

meditating child

being awoken in the dark –
eyes not open –
far from being asleep –

the ocean in the middle
of nowhere – no boundaries
or thought – just seamless-
-ness – open echo –

the sensation
of the realness
in myself –
this is how it felt like.

this was how it felt
not being scared
or second-guessing
being so alone.

although i knew
through these walls,
the room's and my own,
there were other bodies
breathing.

this was how it felt
for once, not inhabiting
in me the sound
of my mother struggling.

only the static
of the night. electricity
running through me.

her pain wanted saving.

tourmaline

ironically,
this coordinate
was what she gave me.

jawe

i don't let my jaw
hang open enough
to show the awe
that i am in
from that
which moves me.
is that why half
of it resides in
the other word;
to phonetically
remind us to be
raw, to drop into
being physically
and sensationally
awe-nest?

insert here

i used to slip
a disc of dreams
into my head
and play it on repeat.

i don't anymore.

into a sieve

everyday we are asked
to empty ourselves.
from last night's images.
from words that obscure
the wordless.
from all that we keep holding on to
as a means to survive.

everyday we are asked
to empty ourselves
into a sieve, and to ask
of ourselves, what stays
and what has to leave.

the blemishes in our stories
we keep repeating to ourselves.
the forgotten treatises
we've unconsciously written,

keeping us from entering
into grander territory,
where there is only us

and usser us.

deluminator

it's time to take back your identity
from all the pockets of people
you've hidden and stored them in.

your mother who you wanted to please.
your father who you wanted to stay.
the multiple friends, lovers, and strangers,
whom you've all wanted to save.

there is strength, resilience,
and love left over
from your attempts to desperately instill
them in others. to reinvest
in yourself;

it is not yet emaciated in you
from trying to live solely
through their eyes.

this reel that you can tap into –
quietly, bit by bit unshackling
from all the center parts of lives
you got lost in, all the doorways
of facial nuances you unconsciously
stepped and resided in –
has a light attached to the end of its hook.

a light that is your own,
a light you had let go,
a light that needs your welcome
to gravitate back
into the place
it belongs most.

ash

all the stars
and all the galaxies
and black holes
and nebulas

stir around
like the ash
of a great bird,
incinerated.

from the corner
of mind's eye
can one only see
what is not quite shown:

we are fragments
of what is burning
to be born again,
to surrender, and fly back home.

landscapes

gardening is a useless endeavor
in a place where boulders
make flourishing impossible.

life becomes empty when we
begin to fill up our world
with ones we don't live in
any longer. or have ever.

there are landscapes in your mind
you've come to comb
a hundred billion times over
that don't rest long enough
for new things to take residence.

you say the past is a ghost
that keeps on haunting you.
but you're the one
who wants the companion.

subconsciously finding comfort
in the dwelling of these pains
you fight to dissipate anyhow.

it's you
who needs to leave it behind –

***

orange ball of alchemy

you will pull yourself through
when you have let yourself
become wholly stuck –

the perception may be
that you are digging yourself
into a hole. right down to the bottom
of a lonely grave. from people
on the outside trying to look in,
and also, when your mind travels
to these dissociating
viewpoints.

but you know, as i know, that
there are just depths and directions
you are most stubbornly
willing to take.

your illumination is still in the origins
of the seed that molded the earth
that molded the layers
of your skin. take refuge in this.
it will gracefully transfer you
to the other side.

you are gold waiting to be sourced.
you are echoing laughter waiting
to be unfettered in caves.

what at first demands strength
will give you all abiding strength
to resume and presume.

luminescent warmth will trickle.

the potential misconception
of being lost gets shrugged away
once you let the thing you are looking for
find you from
staying completely still.

cocoon here.

out of soot and grime and humanness
is where you are most radiantly
compressed.

***

secrete

if you wish to break free,
you've got to give in
to the breaking of you
into pieces
you can never pick up again.
so that everything
you've ever wished for
can rush right through
the openings and into
the very depths of you.
there is so much
that heals on its own
once you stop trying
to fix every crevice,
thinking you have to be
stronger, faster,
and more invincible this
and the next time around.
you will find that
what you want
is always what you have had.
and that to unshackle your self
from yourself
will fill you to the point
where every secret
secretes out
into a balm –
a remedy you always knew
was yours to use
and share.

self-deprecation

we must learn to tell the difference
between knowing when humor
can heal, and when humor only
entertains the hurt that is still left.
one breathes out and the other one
sits as an enabler in disguise.

voltage

you are always looking
for something
to plug into.

why don't you try for a change
to let yourself be
the something
that the great invisible itself
plugs into.

and let electricity flow.

it may tingle and it may unsettle.
but what stirs
is surely done to
put the stars quietly back into
your hungry bloodstreams.

zz.

un-dense

it takes a skilled man
to emit air
into words
and to surround them
with it
(since they are
quite dense),
to speak
through the universe
inside of him,
to travel each breath
along all the centimeters
of his open throat,
sweeping warmly
through each cilium,
acknowledging
every click of the tongue,
to come to a place
where nothing
and everything
is finely said.

***

loveletter

i saw brown residue
in my pipe
and asked v
what she had smoked.
she said,
a love letter.

i told her that letters have ink on it
and she knows that it's poisonous,
right?

then she remembered.

personal belongings & wrecked ships

to get to where you need
to be going requires
a capacity for lightness.

the trauma of not being allowed
to connect
can play in your head
like something you have to
get right this time
get right this time
get right this time.

but all that these hollow
spots need
is to be watered with
your own love.

there is no such thing
as absolutely needing
closure from all of whom
you've only wished for
real unions with.

iceberg (ii)

you watch as seduction to under the sea
turns into something more than just
fantasy;
and that salty waters
can and do crystallize into
something that maintains its buoyancy
from at first being submerged.

fervor, not fever (ii)

to find yourself in an unreality
that keeps being woven by all
those surrounding you.

this is a declaration
of no longer having the quilt
be repeatedly pulled over your head.

since – it might be a shock to hear –
you are not delirious with the fever
they maintain,

but only
have an infinite fervor
for the richness of life.

passion in a jar

there are stars that revolve
around an unstudied black center,
swinging at 100 miles per second.

there are molecules on my skin
that dance chaotically in heat
when i am involved in something
bringing me closer to my own center.

grand or small, the extremes
of all scales tend to end up
looking roughly the same.

giantess

she was clumsy
and didn't know her own power.

she wanted so badly
to synchronize your heart
with hers.

so she gripped down
and dove straight for the crack-
-ing.

wanted to peer inside,
so she pried you open
to see the light
and the childhood pains.

but all you saw was blood.
and all you heard was the thunder
you thought came to claim.

she was clumsy with her honesty.
and you were too easily
scared away.

***

choose to be worthy of taking up space

let go of the idea
that you
are too heavy
for this earth.
let your foot fall
onto the ground,
and stomp –
letting the ground
resound
up unto you.

field of blossoms

i know you hunger
for something so much more,
but it is this stillness
that will settle the waters,
making it clearer
as to what you are looking for.

you just need to learn
to weather the calm
as you have the many storms.
because there is much gold
to be found

when you do not have much
to do,
and when you do not have anything
to prove.

it is a privilege to be able
to stand before the gates of love
like this. where you can see
through to the other side.
and the tall iron entrance
will immediately
and eagerly swing wide,

just as soon as you are able
to pull back the curtains,
dissipate the illusions
that says:
this vibrant field of blossoms,
inches in front of you,
isn't already in the chambers
of where your heart resides.

***

collecting fuel

deep slumber.
necessary hibernation.
walking out to
click mental memories
of sun skies,
and the song on the radio
that coincides
with the voice in your head
urging you
to not give up.
so you post them on walls
and you walk a little further
out into the woods,
where the people sing,
where the animals observe,
where the air bombards
all your senses
in the most monumental way;
filling the deep regions
in your heart to give way.
with each white and pink
flower you harvest on the way
as decoration for your bedpost.
memorabilia to intertwine
in your dreams.
where sleep unties
the many knots
on your patient heartstrings.
and then it passes,
and it's a passage –
these snapshots of collected fuel
for your unassuming venture,
they undulate to unfurl
the moss growing in the damp,
with your feet
more and more in the wetlands –

waiting for you to melt, to become
for a moment, a mirrored pool,
in which only when it is calm
and dark,
can you see yourself
reflecting
the cosmic night sky.

***

stars and moon

on the darkest nights
is when i can see you
most clearly.

time spent chasing
incandescence
through blinding
fluorescence –

i have missed you
so dearly.

emotional charms

you are overdue to step out
of the shadow of fear
of your parents and grandparents,
and your great, great, great ancestors,

whom you've never met
but only know...
through this gnawing sense
of having to stay small to get by.

what you don't know
is that this chain
was built for us to have –
to be able
to be never repeated again;

all looped ends
gives us the choice
to risk dangling off
like newfound charms.

once you can dip into
the colors
of your expansive expressiveness.

see, you can afford
to feel and be everything...
because feigning nothing
has already been tried and not true.

make no mistake:
you are not no one. you are just
not one thing.
you are too many things.

***

and it is possible… that you're saying
you don't know who you are
is that leftover residue
masking the frightening magnitude
of not who you will become, but who
you already are.

adjacent kingdom

don't let yourself be ruled
by the love that was unnourished.
unmet. and unable
to give you free reign
of your adjacent kingdom.

not one person will know how
to follow you completely
into your own mysteries
and the unraveling
of your own bubble.

so try not to shun this failure
either; it will come to be
an adjacent universe aiding you
into your own again –

the friction of a memory
sparking up something anew.
the nudge of soft whispering
winds if you let it. reminding you
how storms can leave their remnants too –

a gift of how calm
it can continue to be
if you let yourself remain on track.
by letting all the gradients
run their course. paralleled
with who is and who is not
on the sides of you.

***

you can't afford to let someone else's
cries, desperation, inattention,
fears, urges to control, or self-absorption
absorb you right along into it.
you can't afford to let a neighboring
presence overwhelm, overpower
or overthrow your foundation.

let your authority be heeded
louder than the one
who ever tries to undermine you.

string theory

vibrations
are the compacting
of all extremes
at its shortest
possible length
from one another.
detailing
a fluctuation
between each
and every side
without adhering
to any.
contradicting,
radical
love.

mystical settling

it will take you a while to get used to
being in the benign warmth
of your own body again.

it will take some restless nights
fighting sleep until you get used to
being in the soothing dark again.

it will take some gentleness
from your own touch to not close
the gaps of anxieties or desires,

but to let the mystical part of your form
perfume out from you, like a waking genie
emerging from its thousand-year-old lamp.

infatuations

wrap up the universe
you have inside yourself,
stirring with feelings,
ready to explode
at the unknowingness
of what may or may not
come from it.
wrap it up…

…and give it away
to be transformed
into a gift, conveying information,
of what has been evoked in you,
to let do with it what they will, perhaps
even stopping that spinning compass
in them, that impasse of their own.
at least you will know.

heart roots

we need the murkiness of soil
for our roots so that we can grow tall.

we need deep sea diving so that we can find
novelty to bring up to the surface.

listen to how your heart wants to sit
heavy on your chest and feel all the rhythms

it wants you to express, however high
or low. sink into yourself and the world.

from dust to dawn

city buildings
will all become
speckled dust.

don't let the prospect
of something having
an end to its phase
hold you back from
giving all you have
to give in the moment.

respect each season.

we mustn't be stingy
with saving and collecting.
reserving for what isn't here yet.
when what is near can only
be built upon all that you
are learning to do *now*.
starting from sand to castle.

eventually we all use
the dust from finished things
left by us, around us,
to build back upper again.

the art of choosing what chooses you

if the thing that you need most
keeps knocking on your door,
you need to see it for what it is,
and to learn the art
of inviting something in.

you need to grow brave enough
to choose what is choosing you too.
and to sit with the strangeness
that needs proper rest on your couch.
this is how the mending begins.

otherwise, you will spend your days
in ignorance, wondering
just why the fuck
that aggravating noise
is not leaving you alone.

the worst of it (ii)

the worst of it is over.

but why settle for the mundane
and why settle for complacency.
as if because the rush
of what the havoc gave is gone now,
the rush of what it means to feel
any exuberance has to too.
as if life wholly got sucked out from you.

that wasn't life, you fool,
that was p o i s o n.

***

sustenance

what we can take comfort in
is the great difference of degrees
we will always come to turn.

these magnetic pole flips
we can't predict or defend against.
these far and farther treks
around the world that may only end up
circling back
to a skin's distance
of where we were at.

but with greater hindsight
and observation.

you see, there is no good or bad
on the scale between elation
or the high tides of despair;
to feel heaven can help us settle
back here at home, and to know
the undulation of heavy tears
allows passage for our possible
baptism.

what we can value is all the shades
of emotions we are offered to taste.
what we are challenged with
is to harness
an equilibrium,
born from the gratefulness
of at least being fed,
and choosing more so
to be full.

imprint

he opened up
the lock
i did not know
i had
into the realms
of something
that made all
the sense;
years of imagery
fixated on
that opening
where the glimpse
of potential
freedom
was mapping
my way
back home.

unsticking the masks (ii)

you will resurface
for good one day.

you will learn
to become the sea.

no longer hiding,
no longer just
a buoy.

shape shifter

there is a melody
that only you can hear
that is the cadence made up
from the sole vibration of you.

the more we lose sight
of whether others can perceive it,
the more the tune gets clearer.

and we will know
not to go back
to trying to be seen, when it only undoes
what we begin to
understand only we can see.

and we will know we were right
then to stop leaning on
the blurry perspective
and the blurry perception
of that which almost blurred us out
of our own existence in the past.

as if we had to prove we were real.

there is new old gravity to be found.
a whole secret symphony to be heard.
that can't be externally measured.
and from that, everything
can form.

***

ripplers

when we can make ripples
with our one little rain drop,

there is a limited space – profound
nonetheless – around us that it can reach.

but when we can grow into a multitude
of drops, a militia of ripplers,

the whole surface of the ocean
can eventually be seen dancing.

until the thunderstorm that is our
love and resilience and magnitude

can pound like the speed of lightening,
connecting us evermore like a stream

between the ground beneath the sea
and the big sky above it all;

we can stretch and heal what time
has confused us to think we cannot.

sun's core

when you live from this space
of tenderness, you live
like how the sun does:
radiating heat that continuously
shines, flickers, moves out
of where it's been, and never
peeks back inside
to try and define and defend
its natural way of being.
it doesn't make itself more
or less than what it is; it just
lives. in touch with its center.

2% light

the sun was never at the center
of our galaxy, and neither is
the light within our human fields.

we are made up of more darkness,
just as the universe is. and that
has always been the foundation
we've been scared to admit
to ourselves, believing that it is
defeat.

that does not mean though that light
is not all around us. it is. it's in
the depths of all the spaces we can
learn to lean into. to widen
our perspectives and be more sound
within our vastness.

a zooming out of our nearsightedness
will have us see there are millions,
if not trillions, of orbs surrounding us.
and we were not meant to only
cling onto the first few we find as if
our lives will fall into a void if we let go.
that void is the inescapable truth
in us, and this gripping makes us
fall short instead to the potential
opening of our souls up against this
eternal night sky,
full of things we can't even possibly
imagine.

light is not currency and when
that can be experienced, it can be abundant.
there is no one source, there is only
an infinite amount
of inner resources.
and when we can settle for that,
we can begin to see
that witnessing beauty
really is the only true god.

peripheries

it may seem at first
that we are tuning out.
tuning out of everything.
but when we intentionally
and have gradually changed
the context of everything –
when we begin to replace
our peripheral attention
of what other people think of us,
and even what we think of ourselves,
with all the physical sensations
reaching out to harmonize
with us, into a chorus within us – that
is when things transform…

and we begin to realize
that what we're actually doing
is tuning in.
maybe for the first time ever.

accumulative

there are some things we just know how
to do, although it seems we've never
gone down that path before.

but the truth is, we have. maybe in our dreams,
or in a past life, or in the wishes of a life
we have most furtively shaped in our hearts.

the memories of all that swirls in the spirals
of our DNA, asking to be unbound, one by one,
as the next possibility arises, and the next.

we don't remember that we've taken the first
step many, many times already. and the fear
of the leap is only in our limited present minds.

we have flown like eagles, written great novels
that have been stored away, fallen from these
heights, and have ventured off to do so much more.

until at last we are here again, looking over the edge.
praying we will land on our own two feet. Yet not
knowing another universe is opening up right below us.

)(